Games
For
Fun

games for fun

MILDRED WADE

BROADMAN PRESS
NASHVILLE, TENNESSEE

Dewey Decimal Classification: 790.1
Subject heading: GAMES

Library of Congress Catalog Card Number: 77-76616
Printed in the United States of America

Contents

1

Get Acquainted
and
Find Partner Games

1. Find Your Own Name and Address. Two boxes are placed near the door where guests will be arriving. One box contains slips of paper with the names of the guests expected to attend; the other contains their addresses. Each guest, as he arrives, pins a slip from each box on his clothing. Guests then move around the room trying to locate their own names and addresses. When a player finds his own name and address, he pins them on himself and pins the ones he's wearing on the guest who has his. Trading continues until everyone in the room has his own name and address pinned to his shirt.

2. Song Titles. Each guest is given the name of a well-known song on a slip of paper as he arrives. Guests are instructed to search for two or three others (depending on size of group) with the same song title. When the groups have found each other, give them a few minutes to prepare their song to sing to the entire group.

3. Autographs. As guests arrive they are given a sheet of paper and a pencil. They are told to mingle with the other guests and get an autograph from each person they talk to. At a given time a prize may be awarded to the person with the longest list of autographs.

4. Four Letter Words. Each player is given a large paper or cardboard with a large letter of the alphabet printed on it. He pins this to his shirt front. At a given signal from the leader, players are to join with other players to form four-letter words. Members forming the first word and showing it to the leader or hostess receive a prize. Others continue the game and a prize is given for the group forming a word last, or no word.

5. Who Am I? Prepare as many name tags as there will be guests. On each name tag write the name of a famous person such as Abraham Lincoln, Chopin, Napoleon, Joan of Arc, and so on. As each guest arrives a name tag is pinned on his back. He is told to find out who he is by asking leading questions such as Am I a man or woman? Living? Dead? Am I an American? Only answers of yes or no may be given. As each guest finds out who he is he may remove his name tag. (Variation of WHO AM I?: If all guests know each other, guests' names may be substituted for famous names. Be sure no one gets his own name.)

6. The Other Half. Write different proverbs on plain cards, one to each card. Cut each proverb in half and put the first half into one box and the second half into another box. When guests arrive the women are given one half a card from one box and the men are given a half from the other box. Guests move around the room until they find the other half of their proverbs and thereby their partners.

7. What's My Smell? Number a piece of paper from one to however many guests there will be. Number down like a list.

Give a copy to each person present. Before guests arrive fill little pill bottles with cotton on which has been put alcohol, different perfumes and lotions (men's and women's), peanut butter, nail polish, vanilla, nail polish remover, liquid floor wax, ammonia, coffee, tea, and so on. As guests arrive give each person a scented bottle with a number on it. Each guest goes to the other guests, asks their names, and tries to identify their bottle scents. Players write names and scents next to corresponding numbers. Player with most correct scents wins.

8. My Name. When all guests have arrived and are seated, the leader begins by saying, for instance, "My name is Mildred and I'm glad to meet you." The person on the right stands and says, "How do you do, Mildred, my name is Hazel." The third person stands and says, "How do you do, Mildred and Hazel, my name is Carl." Game continues until each person has given all other names starting with the first name given and ending with his own name. If a player has difficulty remembering someone's name, he may be prompted by the others but not eliminated from the game.

9. No Smiling, Please. Players are seated in a circle. The leader touches, with his right hand, some part of the face of the player on his left. The leader keeps his finger on that spot as each player, in turn, touches the player on his left. Anyone who laughs must leave the game. Game continues with each person touching a different spot on the next player's face until all have laughed and only one player is left. He is the winner. (Players might touch another player's ear, pull his nose, touch his teeth, pull his hair, etc.)

10. Half and Half. To pair off guests, cut in half as many old

Rook cards (or pictures or valentines, or paper dolls, or magazine ads) as you have pairs of guests. Shuffle the top halves of the cards and give them to the ladies. Give the bottom halves to the men. Instruct the guests to find their "better halves" for the next game or for the evening.

11. Silly Action. Make two slips of paper with one of the following on them: tongue sticker outer, head scratcher, ear puller, thigh slapper, hand shaker, finger snapper, eye winker, foot stomper, knee bender, nose blower, eye rubber, nose twitcher, peace-sign maker, nose scratcher, hair puller, thumb sucker, knock-kneed walker, pigeon-toed walker, side holder, stomach patter, nail biter, sneezer, cougher, etc. Give one half of each pair to the men and one half to the ladies. Then each person moves about the room doing what his paper says until he meets his partner who will be doing the same thing.

2

Indoor Games

12. What's in a Face? Collect a number of pictures of people from illustrated magazines. Select a committee of three judges. Give each player a picture, and felt pens or colored crayons. Each player is to touch up his picture in whatever way he likes. At the end of ten minutes all finished pictures are pinned on the wall for the judges to choose a winner.

13. Name That Tune. Players form two teams and line up single file in each team. The first player in each team stands at a chalk mark on the floor facing a chair at the other end of the room. A record player at the side of the room begins to play. The first player of each team must quickly determine if he knows the name of the record. If he does he puts on a pair of provided bedroom slippers and races to the chair, touches it and calls out the name of the tune. The record is changed with each two players. The team with the most correctly named tunes wins.

14. Name That Product. Cut about twenty advertisements from magazines, being sure to mark out or cut out all names of the products. Pass the numbered pictures among the players for them to write down on their papers next to the corresponding numbers the names of the products.

15. Jerusalem and Jericho. Place players in a line facing the leader. When the leader calls out "Jerusalem," all players must bow deeply. When he calls out "Jericho," no one may move. The leader tries to trick the players by saying the first syllable very slowly and trying to cause some of the players to make a false move. Anyone failing to bow at the right time or bowing at the wrong time is out of the game. After a given time, remaining players win.

16. Coin Game. Team 1 is seated on one side of a table. Team 2 is seated opposite them. Team 1 is "It" and is given a coin which they must pass from player to player under the table. When the leader of Team 2 says, "All hands on table," players on Team 1 put their hands on the table with fists closed. Team 2 goes into consultation and tries to guess which hand holds the coin. Team 2 has as many guesses as there are players on Team 1, less one. If the coin is located within the allowed number of guesses, Team 2 gets the coin. If not, Team 1 scores and keeps the coin for the next try.

17. Whose Nose? Make a hole in an old sheet. The hole should be just large enough for a player to put his nose through. Ask several players to step behind the sheet and show their noses while the other players try to guess whose nose it is. Players may touch the nose sticking through the sheet or otherwise examine it before guessing whose it is.

18. Magic Squares. Arrange nine squares (such as record albums) on the floor or table in this fashion: □ □ □
□ □ □
□ □ □

In advance the leader has told one guest how to play the game. He goes out of the room and the other guests decide which square they want him to guess is their chosen one. The player comes back into the room. The leader points with a pointer, ruler, or yardstick to a square and asks, "Is this it?" until the player says yes. The informed player goes out of the room again while another square is chosen by the group. The informed player continues to guess the right square. This continues until someone "catches on" to how it is done and volunteers to go out of the room while a square is chosen. Game continues until every player "catches on" or gives up.

Trick to the game: Leader gives position of the chosen square to the informed player the first time he points and says, "Is this it?" For instance, if the chosen square is the center one, the leader first places his pointer in the center of a square. If the chosen one is the one at the upper right hand, the leader first places his pointer in the upper right hand corner of any square. After the leader first points and discloses the chosen one, he can then point to any he likes until he's ready to point to the chosen one.

19. Mrs. Johnson's Tea. Players are to discover for themselves the object of the game while playing. The leader begins by saying to the person next to him, "Mrs. Johnson doesn't like tea. Do you know what she likes?" Correct answers may be coffee, milk, or any suitable word not containing the letter "t". If a player answers with a word containing the letter "t" he is out. Players continue asking the person nearest him the above question. Players are at first puzzled but some will soon catch on to the idea that "t" may not be used in any word since it starts the word tea. To throw some players off, the following questions may be substituted: Do you know what she likes to wear? Do you know what entertainment she likes? Do you know her favorite food?

20. Proverbs. All players sit in a circle. One of them throws a small rubber ball at another player. That player must say a well-known proverb before the thrower can count to ten. If he succeeds he becomes the thrower. If he fails, he must pay a forfeit. Proverbs may not be repeated.

21. Clap Hands. One player leaves the room while the other players decide who he is to kneel before upon his return. The kneeler kneels before the various players. He is guided to the chosen one by claps. Loud claps show that he is warm and soft claps indicate he is cold.

22. Bubbles. Each guest is given a piece of bubble gum. All guests begin chewing and trying to blow bubbles. Guest who blows the biggest bubble wins.

23. Quarter Drop. Each player, in turn, places a quarter between his knees, walks to a plastic cup or glass about four feet away and tries to drop the quarter into the cup without using his hands.

24. Listen to This. Players form a circle. Each person, in turn, describes in detail his most embarrassing moment, his pet peeve, his biggest thrill, his most daring adventure, etc., choosing the category he wishes.

25. Clap Seven. Players sit in a circle and count in turn consecutively beginning with the number one. When any player reaches seven or any multiple of seven or a number containing the number seven, he must not say the number but clap his hands once instead. When a player forgets to clap his hands at the proper time or if he says the forbidden numbers, he is out of the game and the game starts over again and continues until only one player is left.

26. The Jester. Players are seated on the floor in a circle. The "jester" stands before any player in the circle he chooses and says or does anything he likes to make the player laugh. The "jester" may not touch any player in the circle. "Jester" continues with each player in the circle until one laughs. Any player who laughs must leave the circle and the last one remaining wins.

27. Crackers. Give each player three crackers. At a given signal all players eat their crackers. The first player to whistle wins the game.

28. Who's Got the Ring? Players stand in a circle, each grasping with both hands a long, continuous string which has been knotted to make a circle. The string has a ring on it. The ring is passed from player to player along the string. Every effort is made to keep the ring hidden at all times. For instance players may pretend to be passing the ring when they don't have it. "It" stands in the center of the circle. At his given command of "Stop" all hands stop moving. "It" then points to the hand he thinks is holding the ring. If he is correct, that person becomes "It." If he is incorrect he continues the game until he does locate the ring.

29. Horner in the Corner. One player is selected to be "Horner" and stands in the middle of the room. The other players stand in the four corners of the room. No player may remain in a corner past the time it takes for the leader to count to twenty. The game is played by one player beckoning another to change places. While they are changing, Horner makes a rush for one of the unoccupied corners. The player he replaces in the corner becomes Horner.

30. Fruit Basket. Place chairs in a circle, one for all players except one. Players sit in chairs with "It" in the center. Each person is given the name of a fruit by "It." "It" calls out (for example), "Orange and pear change places." While they are changing "It" tries to sit in one of the vacant chairs. When he succeeds the ousted one becomes "It."

31. Words Without Music. Select a number of well-known hymns or songs. From each write down one line except the first line. Each player, in turn, is read one line. He must then sing the entire song from the beginning. Suggestions:

Who yielded his life an atonement for sin—To God Be the Glory

Lose all their guilty stains—There is a Fountain

There to my heart was the blood applied—Down at the Cross

32. The Maze. Use colored ribbons or strings (one color for boys; the other color for girls) to make the maze as difficult or as easy as the leader desires. On one end of each ribbon or string tie a small gift. All gifts are placed on a table which is centrally located. Then the leader strings the ribbons or strings, one at a time, all over the house (or room), around and under tables, chairs, and other furniture. The free ends of the ribbons or strings are brought together at a starting point. Each player is to take one of the free ends and follow his ribbon or string wherever it may lead him until he comes to his gift at the other end of the ribbon or string. (Keep gifts

16

simple and inexpensive such as note pads, pencils, etc.)

33. Hot and Cold Music. A player is chosen to leave the room while other players hide an object. The first player is then called in and told what the object is that he must find. The other players help him by singing a tune. When the player approaches the hiding place the music grows louder; as he goes away from the object the music grows softer.

34. Odd Man Out. Arrange chairs in a double row with the chairs standing back to back and facing in opposite directions. There should be one less chair than there are players. The players line up around the chairs and march around them as the music plays. When the music stops everyone dashes for a chair to sit in. The one left without a chair is out of the game. A chair is removed and the music begins again, and again stops suddenly. Every time a player is eliminated a chair is removed until there remains a contest between two players vying for one chair.

35. Spinning Plate. One person is placed in the center of a circle of other players. As the person spins a tin pie plate he calls out the name of one of the players. The one whose name is called must jump up and catch the plate before it stops spinning. If he fails, he goes back to the circle and the first one spins again, calling another name. If this player catches the plate it is his turn to spin it. (If players do not know each other well, numbers can be given for names.)

36. Barnyard. Hide about thirty nuts (or beans) throughout the room. Divide the guests into small groups who choose their own leaders. Assign to each group an animal sound such as cow, dog, turkey, etc. All players search for

17

the nuts (or beans) but only the leaders may pick them up. When a player locates a nut (or bean) he must make the sound of the animal assigned to his group to attract the attention of his leader who comes and collects the nut. The group finding the most nuts wins.

37. Heads or Tails. Players are divided into two teams, the Heads and the Tails. Teams face each other about two feet apart. The leader tosses a coin and calls out the side that turns up. If it comes up heads, the Heads team must laugh aloud while the Tails team keep straight faces. The Heads team tries to make the Tails team laugh. All who do must join the other team and the coin is tossed again.

38. Do As I Do. Sitting in a circle the first player does something for all players to see, such as touching his ear. The second player touches his ear and adds an action of his own such as clapping his hands. The third player does the above two and adds one of his own, in order. Each player continues in like manner. When one player makes a mistake by performing one of the actions out of sequence or forgets an action, he is out of the game. Game continues until only one remaining in the game can accurately perform actions.

39. View the Legs. In advance hang a sheet so that the bottom of sheet comes to the knee area. With the women out of the room, the men remove their shoes, roll their pants legs up to the knee, and stand behind the sheet. Women enter the room and try to guess which pair of legs belong to their husbands. Another version of this is for the men to stand behind the sheet with only their bare feet showing and the wives guess as before.

18

40. Toilet Paper. Leader passes a roll of toilet tissue to players one at a time with the instruction to take the length he wants. When all have taken the tissue, the leader states that the one who has a piece that fits his waistline wins.

41. Clothes Pin. Each woman is given a clip-on clothes pin. Reaching between her legs she clips her pin on the back of her dress as high as she can reach. One with highest pin wins.

42. Baby Pictures. Each guest brings a baby picture of himself which will be returned. Pictures are mounted by one person on a large board and numbered. Each player writes who he thinks the baby pictures are next to the corresponding numbers on paper.

43. Change Seats. All players sit in chairs arranged in a circle. One is selected to be "It" and stands in the middle, leaving his chair vacant. "It" calls out, "Shift to the right." All players move one chair to the right and sit down. "It" tries to get a seat. During the move to the right "It" may suddenly call out "Shift to the left." In the confusion "It" may get a seat and the player left without a seat becomes "It."

44. Stack Up. Hostess should have a supply of empty paper cupcake containers. Each guest, in turn, stacks the containers in a single stack. Player with the highest number of containers in his stack wins.

45. Never on Time. Form an equal team of men and women, to find out why the men say they have to wait on the women to go out, and vice versa. Women are given a suitcase of men's clothing and men are given a suitcase of women's clothing. Each player, in turn, puts on the outfit, turns around for everyone to see, removes clothes and puts them back in suitcase and gives it to the next person on the team. Team finishing first wins. Suggested clothing (all oversized): Men—underpants, bra, slip, dress, gloves, hat, purse; Women—undershorts, undershirt, shirt, trousers, belt, hat.

46. What's in an Egg? Make a small hole (dime size or smaller) in an egg and remove the egg white and egg yolk. After eggshell has dried, insert items you find around the house such as: needle, golf tee, hairpin, nail, thread, pin, hook and eye, stamp, olive, nut, coin, toothpick, button, raisin, seed, cube of bread, etc. (about fifty items). Ask guests to list on their papers all the things they think might be found in the eggshell that can be found around the house. After all have written their lists, remove items from egg. Give one point for each correct item.

47. Musical Hands. Players are divided into two teams. Each secretly chooses a tune. The first team claps out the rhythm of its chosen tune which the second team must guess. If the second team is unable to identify the tune, the first team gets another turn, otherwise the second team claps out its chosen tune for the first team to guess.

48. Name the Articles. Before guests arrive select about thirty articles, such as a sponge, an eggbeater, bottle opener, etc. Players are seated in a circle. Turn out the lights and pass around the articles, one by one. Players feel the articles and pass them on to the next person. When all articles have been around, hostess collects them and turns lights back on. Guests are then given pencils and papers and asked to name as many articles as they can remember. Player with the longest list of correct names wins.

49. Step Carefully. Each player is blindfolded in turn and brought into a room where he is told eggs have been placed in his path. He is instructed to walk carefully so as not to step on the eggs. Hostess carefully heads him in direction of eggs. Actually crackers have been placed in floor instead of eggs. (Crackers being stepped on sound like eggs being stepped on.)

50. Family Coach. Players are seated in a circle. The leader assigns to each the name of something connected with the family coach; for example, driver, horses, wheel, axle, reins, whip, spoke, nut, door, bridle, bit, passengers, footman, mother, father, children, grandma, food, etc. The hostess has prepared in advance a dramatic story dealing with a trip in the family coach. As each word or name is spoken, the person to whom it has been assigned must stand up, turn around, and sit down again. When family coach is mentioned everyone must stand up and whirl around. The leader tries to get a seat. If he succeeds the one left without a chair must continue reading the story and the leader becomes his name.

51. Ghosts. The leader begins by naming a letter of the alphabet. The player next to him adds a letter, thinking of some word. Each player in turn must add a letter, but must not make a complete word. If he does finish a word he becomes a half ghost and the other players may not speak to him. Any player who does speak to him also becomes a half ghost. The half ghosts may continue talking and playing.

When a word has been finished the next player starts a new word with a single letter. If a half ghost finishes a word he becomes a whole ghost and is out of the game but still may talk. If any player talks to him that player becomes a full ghost. Game continues until all players have been eliminated.

52. Famous People. "It" is chosen and goes into another room while the others think of a famous person. When "It" is called back he is told the first letter of the famous person's last name. "It" must try to find out who the famous person is by asking questions. Questions must be asked of each person in turn and must be correctly answered. For instance if the players thought of Roosevelt "It" may ask, "Is he a famous ball player?" "It" may ask the second player, "Is she a woman?" "It" continues around the circle of players until he guesses. Any player who incorrectly answers a question must pay a forfeit. If "It" cannot guess the famous person in one round he gives up and another player takes his place.

53. Famous Names. One player starts the game by saying, "I know a famous person whose name begins with a B (for Beethoven). Players guess at random until the right person is named. Player who guesses correctly begins with another name.

54. Emotions. "It" stands in the middle of a circle of players and names some emotion such as anger, pity, fear, surprise, grief, sorrow, joy, etc. He closes his eyes and counts to ten. While he is counting players must assume facial expressions and poses to portray the emotion named. "It" opens his eyes and decides which player has best portrayed the emotion. He becomes "It."

55. Geography. Players sit in a circle and one person is selected to be "It." "It" says, "I am going to Algiers." The next player must spell Algiers correctly and continue the journey any place he likes. When a player misspells a place he becomes "It." The original "It" may get his seat back if he can spell correctly the place, otherwise he is out of the game.

56. Colored Squares. Cut colored construction paper in 3-inch squares (or any size). Give each player two squares each of six different colors (black, green, pink, yellow, blue, white). Players are given ten minutes to trade their colored squares any way they want to such as a black for a blue or two white for a green, etc. After the trading is done, tell the players the value of each color such as: black, five points; green, ten; pink, fifteen; yellow, twenty; blue, thirty; white, forty. Player with highest number of points wins.

57. United States. Players are seated in a circle. One is selected to be "It." "It" points to any player, calls out the name of a state, and counts to ten. The person pointed to must give the name of a city in that state before "It" finishes counting. If he cannot name a city in that state he becomes "It" and must take his place in the center.

58. True or False. In advance prepare a list of facts such as those below, some true, some false. Place the players in a straight line down the center of the room. Designate one side of the room True and one side False. Each fact is read aloud to the players who decide quickly if the fact is true or false and then run to that side of the room. The correct answer to each fact is then read and those who have made a mistake must pay a forfeit.

Sunday is the first day of the week . . . . T
"Cleanliness is next to Godliness" is in the Bible . F
New Jersey is the smallest state . . . . F
Pocahontas married John Rolfe . . . . T
A drowning person rises three times . . . . F
Bats are blind . . . . F
Fish is a brain food . . . . F
Delano is President Roosevelt's middle name . . . . T
A piece of standard typing paper is 8½
x 11 inches . . . . T
Peach pits are larger than avocado pits . . . . F

59. Find the Treasures. Select thirty objects such as a match, pencil, nut, button, etc. and hide them in different places about the room. Conceal them as skillfully as possible so they can be seen without moving anything but be easily overlooked. For instance, a safety pin might be placed in an ashtray, a toothpick may be placed on the quarter round, etc. Each guest is to take his list as he walks around the room looking for objects and writes down their hiding places as he finds them without letting the other guests know where he has found an object. Person finding the most objects wins.

60. Actors and Audience. Divide players into two groups, one the actors and the other the audience. Actors leave the room while the audience selects a word such as "sew." The actors are called in and told that the word rhymes with "go." Actors try to guess the word which must be acted out. They may think it is "hoe" and start to hoe. The audience shakes their heads no and the actors act out another word until they get it right. Audience and actors change places. The group that guesses its word correctly with the least number of attempts is the winner.

61. Coffeepot. One player is sent out of the room while the other players decide upon a word that represents some kind of activity. The player is called back into the room and tries to find out what the activity is by asking questions of any player. He must use the word coffeepot to represent the activity. Suppose riding a bicycle was chosen as the activity. The person may ask, "Do you coffeepot?" "When do you coffeepot?" "Do you coffeepot at night?" All questions must be answered truthfully because the answers furnish the clues to more questions. The player who gives the answer enabling the questioner to guess the activity is the next one sent out of the room while the group thinks of another activity.

62. Potato Stocking. Put a potato in the toe of a stocking. Tie that stocking in the center to two more stockings that have been tied together to make one length. Tie stocking length around player's chest. By swinging the potato stocking between legs, the player tries to knock another potato on the floor as far as possible. The player knocking the potato on the floor the farthest distance wins.

63. Necktie Game. Select five or six shy men and have them come to the center of the group or in front of the group. Then tell them they must sing a song, kiss someone's wife, or anything they would be reluctant to do. Instruct them, one at a time to carry out your orders. In advance of the social, cue one man in on how you plan to conduct the game and call on him first. Tell him to sing a song (or whatever you decide on). He should refuse. Then tell him that if he doesn't sing a song you will cut off his necktie. Hold the scissors up to his tie to show that you mean it. Tell him again to sing. He again refuses. Then actually cut off his tie near the knot. (Being aware of how the game goes, he will have worn an old tie.) Then tell each man, in turn, to sing a song. Chances are each man will sing rather than have his necktie cut off.

64. Magic Selection. The leader needs a confederate who knows how to play the game. The confederate goes out of the room. Meanwhile the others decide on some object in the room for him to guess such as a table. When the confederate returns, the leader points to various objects in turn and asks the confederate if that is the object. Leader points to several objects before he points to the right one. The confederate guesses it is the table. The secret to the game is that the leader points to something white immediately before pointing to the selected object. Any player who thinks he has a clue to how the game is played may go out of the room and try his luck. The game is more fun if those who think they have guessed how to play keep their clues to themselves.

65. Story Telling. Assign a letter of the alphabet to each player. If there are more than twenty-six players, start with the letter A again. Each person is to think of an adjective beginning with the letter he has been given. In the order of the alphabet, players inject their adjectives into a narrative the leader reads slowly, pausing for words to be given. Example narrative: An "angry" group of "bad" members from the "carnivorous" First Baptist Church met for a

26

"D" time at an "E" birthday party for their "F" minister. The one for whom the "G" party was given was the "H" Bill Jones. He and his "I" wife, Jane, were surprised at attending a "J" party. They thought they were coming to a "K" meeting with other "L" leaders of the "M" church. The "N" members were disappointed that their "O" minister's "P" children were unable to attend but they were in the "Q" nursery with the "R" workers. Brother Bill uses a "S" technique in delivering his "T" sermons, but the "V" congregation, "W" choir, and "X" deacons think his sermons are "Y" all the time and "Z" some of the time.

66. For Women Only or Men Only. A person is selected for "It" and is told to sit in the middle of the room. A blanket is placed gently over her head. She then is told to take off everything she doesn't need. (The blanket is what she doesn't need but she will probably take off shoes, rings, watch, etc., etc., etc.)

67. Not "I." Each player is given ten clip-on clothespins that he clips to his clothing. During the entire evening (or a specified time of about an hour), if a player uses the word "I" he must give one of his pins to the person who first called his attention to the fact that he used the word. At the end of the game the player with the most pins wins.

68. Don't Cross. A small gift is given to one member present. He is told he may keep the gift if he doesn't cross his legs at the knee or ankle. If he does cross his legs he must give the gift to whoever catches him doing it. Game continues in this manner for entire evening or for a specified period of time of at least an hour. At the end of the evening the person with the gift keeps it.

69. Follow Directions. Players form a circle and the leader tells them to hold their left ear with their right hand and hold their nose with their left. Give ample time for everyone to achieve this pose. Then the leader calls out "Reverse." Those who do not do this quickly are eliminated from the game which continues until only one player is left. (A variation of this game is to have players rub the tops of their heads with the right hand and pat their stomachs with the left. Then reverse as before.)

70. Sardines. All rooms are left open for this game and the lights are turned out. One player hides. As each player finds the hidden person, he joins him without making a sound. This continues until all are packed in the hiding place like sardines. The last one to find the hidden person pays a forfeit. Game then begins again.

71. Taking a Trip. Players sit in a circle. One begins the game by saying, "I am going to Jerusalem. I'll take an umbrella." The next player says, "I am going to Jerusalem. I'll take an umbrella and a coat." Each player takes his turn repeating all the articles said before and adding one of his own. If a player misses an article or changes the sequence, he is out of the game but remains in his seat. Other players continue until only one is left.

72. Pucker Up. Leader tells the men she is taking the ladies out of the room for a minute to talk them into giving the men a kiss. When the women return, they line up facing the men (not their own husbands) who are told to close their eyes, pucker up, and the women will give them a kiss. As each man finally opens his eyes to see why he hasn't been given his kiss, the women facing them hand them a Hershey chocolate kiss.

3

Outdoor Games

73. Tom Tiddler's Ground. An area of the playground is marked off as Tom Tiddler's Ground and Tom sits within the area apparently asleep. The other players must cross over the boundary saying, "We are on Tom Tiddler's Ground picking up gold and silver." They continue crossing over the boundary line until Tom wakens and makes a dash for them. Tom must not cross the boundary line, however. Any player he catches takes Tom's place.

74. Blow the Whistle. All players except two hold hands and form a circle. (If circle needs to be larger, players take one or two steps backward.) One of the remaining players is blindfolded and the other player is given a whistle. These two are placed inside the circle. The blindfolded player tries to catch the other player who blows his whistle every now and then to signal where he is and dodges about trying not to be caught. When he is caught he is blindfolded and another player is chosen to take his place and use the whistle.

75. Balloon Stamp. With string tie a blown-up balloon to each ankle of each player. At a given signal everyone stamps on the others' balloons to make them burst. Person left with a balloon wins.

76. Waken Rip Van Winkle. One, two, or three (depending on size of group) players lie down and pretend to be asleep. All other players steal up to the "sleepers" and touch them. Sleepers waken, jump up and catch as many players as they can before leader blows a whistle or calls time from a stop watch. Those caught become the sleepers and game continues.

77. Teacher. All players stand in a line facing one who is "Teacher." "Teacher" throws a basketball to the player at the head of the line who throws it back. "Teacher" then throws the ball to the next player, and so on down the line. Any player who misses the ball goes to the end of the line. If "Teacher" misses the ball he must also go to the end of the line, and the player at the head of the line takes his place.

78. Catch Kitty. All players are blindfolded except "Kitty" who is given a little bell to ring. The blindfolded players must try to catch "Kitty" as he moves about ringing his bell. The player who catches "Kitty" becomes the new "Kitty" and the game continues.

79. Balloon Toss. Select one player to be "It." All other players are seated on the ground in a circle and each is given a number. "It" throws the balloon (or handkerchief) in the air and calls out a number. The player whose number is called must catch the balloon before it touches the floor. If he fails to catch the balloon he becomes "It." (Extra balloons may be needed.)

80. Ball Game. Have an equal number in each team. Each of the two teams forms a line facing the other team with a space of about three feet between them. Place a chair at each end of the space between the teams. One chair is goal for team A and the other chair is goal for team B. The first player of each team stands in the center of the two teams and a ball is placed between the brooms (one per team). Object is to push the ball (no bigger than a basketball) under respective goal (chair). After one team has scored, next two players compete. Scorekeeper determines which team makes most goals.

81. Scavenger Hunt. Prepare in advance a list of articles for each group (two to five players) to obtain, even if they must go door to door. All groups leave with a list at a given time and are instructed to return at a given time with the articles. Time limit may be anywhere from one to three hours. Winning group brings back most items. Suggested list of things to be hunted:

burned-out light bulb	carpet tack
toenail	valentine
piece of rye bread	paper clip
gray hair	potato peeling piece
red toothpick	broken cup
worn out toothbrush	shoe with hole in sole
grain of corn	paper cup
old calendar	dead flashlight battery
eggshell piece	red hair
prune	pencil stub
3-week-old church bulletin	rusty nail
red yarn piece	chicken bone
bill of sale for anything	yellow button
empty Clorox bottle	raisin

baby aspirin
old stamp
old telephone directory
soap wrapper
empty Listerine bottle
lavender toilet tissue
piece of hardened nail
    polish
green thread

red ribbon
signature of a nurse
hairnet
poster
week-old newspaper
empty tomato soup can
hair from a horse
piece of macrame

4

Pencil and Paper Games

82. Music Box. A pianist is necessary who can play a number of songs from memory. As the pianist plays each song in rapid succession, players write down the names of the songs as quickly as possible. The winner is the player who gets the largest number of song titles correct.

83. Artist. Each player is given pencil and paper and instructed to draw a picture, in order, in the dark: A lake, a canoe in the lake, a man in the canoe, a fishing pole in the man's hand, a fish on the fishing line, and a moon in the sky.

84. Unscramble. On strips of paper write familiar Bible verses or proverbs. Make an identical set for each group of five or six players. Cut each strip into three or four pieces. Each group should spread the pieces out in plain sight on a table and rearrange them to make complete Bible verses or proverbs. Group completing theirs first wins.

85. Grand Slam. Each player is given pencil and paper and instructed to write as many words as he can in five minutes to describe the guest of honor (or anyone).

86. Story Telling. Pencils and paper are distributed among the players. The game begins with everyone writing down an adjective describing a woman. Each paper is folded down about one half inch and passed to the player on the right. Each player now writes down the name of a woman and passes his paper to the right again. This continues until there has been written an adjective describing a man, a man's name, where they met, what she wore, what he wore, what she did, what he did, what she said, what he said, the consequences, and what the world said. Papers are then read aloud in turn by each player with the necessary words being inserted to give the story continuity.

87. Only One Word. Give each guest a paper and pencil. They are to write down the following letters as the leader calls them out in this order: D, N, W, E, O, N, O, R, O, Y, L. At a signal to begin guests are told to arrange these letters so they spell only one word. The first guest to come up with "Only One Word" wins.

88. Blind Pig. One player is blindfolded and seated at a table. He is given a large sheet of paper and a pencil and told to draw a pig. He must begin with the ears and add the tail last. Each guest takes his turn. When every guest has drawn his pig, a prize is given for the best drawing. You might like to give a prize for the worst drawing also.

89. Fabric. In advance prepare a booklet of construction paper for each guest (size, about four inches square; stapled). The eight pages in the booklet should be labeled with one of the following sets of words on each page: Seen in the newspaper, What housewives should be, A sign of mourning, As good as cash, What sheep produce, A certain kind of cheese, Part of the flag, What fishermen use. Each player is provided with an envelope containing one one-inch square of the following cloth or fabric: black, checks, wool, dotted swiss, print, domestic, striped, net. At a given signal each player tries to match the appropriate type of fabric with the appropriate set of words. First player to complete his booklet correctly wins. Answers: Seen in the newspaper, print; What housewives should be, domestic; Sign of mourning, black; As good as cash, checks; What sheep produce, wool; A kind of cheese, swiss; Part of the flag, stripes, What fishermen use, net.

90. Five Minutes. The leader instructs players to write down as many names of vegetables as they can beginning with the letter "B" for instance. At the end of five minutes the first player reads his list aloud. Other players cross out the duplicates on their lists. Then the other players in turn read their lists while other players cross out duplicates. Only those names remaining which were not listed by any other player count in the scoring of one point for each. Leader then selects another letter for words and instructs players to name trees, flowers, cities, etc. Player with the highest score wins.

91. Predictions. Each player writes his name on a piece of paper, folds it and puts it in a box. In turn, each player draws another player's name and writes a prediction for that person for the next ten years. When finished, predictions are passed, so that no one reads his own, and read.

92. Rhymes. The first person in a circle writes down the first line of a rhyme. He then folds down the paper so that his line doesn't show and passes the paper to the person on his right, telling him only the last word of the line. That person writes another line ending with a word rhyming with the last word of the line preceding. Each time the paper is folded so that the writing doesn't show, and passed to the person on the right telling only the last word written. When the paper has gone around the circle it is unfolded and read aloud.

93. Telegrams. Guests are given ten letters of the alphabet to write down as they are dictated. Each guest is to compose a telegram of ten words, each word beginning with one of the letters in the dictated order. Allow ten minutes and then ask each guest to read his telegram. The game is more fun if telegrams are to be written for a designated occasion such as birthday, marriage proposal, etc.

94. Ten Pennies. Each player is given ten pennies, paper and pencil. Each player writes ten ordinary or common things he has never done (such as eat strawberry ice cream or ride an escalator). Each person in turn reads his list aloud. For everything on his list that no one else has, everyone gives him a penny. After all lists have been read, person with most pennies wins. Everyone keeps the pennies he is left with.

95. Fruits, Flowers, and Trees. The leader scrambles the names of flowers, trees, and fruits which form odd phrases and sentences. Guests are to write the correct names beside the scrambled ones. Examples:

On a tin car (carnation) O my cares (sycamore)
I'd say (daisy) Go near (orange)
Ah, Lida (dahlia) A green egg (greengage)

Read Noel (oleander)

A long aim (magnolia)

Old man (almond)
I love (olive)
Many a hog (mahogany)

Bees rise or go (gooseberries)

O grant me, Ape! (pomegranate)

He paces (peaches)
O anger! (orange)

96. Great Expectations. Supply each player with paper and pencil. Instruct them to write what they expect from their new pastor, boss, newlywed (or anyone). No one signs his paper. Papers are passed until hostess says to stop. Each person then reads the paper he is holding.

97. Love Story. Give out papers on which has been written the following, leaving space for the blanks to be filled in with the words at the bottom of the paper.

When ____ shot his ____ on ____ Day a new ____ affair began. The ____ started with a ____ with a beautiful ____ in it. A few days later a ____ and ____ lacy box of ____ arrived in the mail. But the ____ of red ____ let me know that we were now ____. The ____ developed into a beautiful romance and we were ____ in a quiet little church service. The exchange of ____ made my ____ skip a beat. Red ____ and ____ are traditions of February 14.

Words: Arrow, love, poem, letter, romance, cupid, valentines, bouquet, candy (2), white, red, married, rings, heart, crush, roses (2), sweethearts.

Person finishing correctly first wins.

98. Trade Gifts. Each player is given three pieces of paper. On one he writes his name, on another his address, and on the other, his phone number. All papers are folded

37

and placed in a box or hat. (Leader has bought gifts in advance—one gift for every three or four guests.) Leader pulls out one paper and reads it. Player whose name, address or phone number is on it gets a gift. Leader continues reading papers, one at a time. Each player, when his name, address or phone number is called, gets a gift. He may select one of the remaining gifts or he may select any gift any player has already opened. When leader's gifts are gone and game continues, players may select gifts from other players. After all papers have been read, players holding gifts keep them.

99. Point Game. Leader gives out pencil and paper and instructs players to write down the designated number of points for each thing they're wearing:

nail polish—10 points
lace on anything—5
brown shoes—10
handkerchief (not tissue)—15
jewelry, each piece—5
zipper—5
buckles on shoes—10
leather or cloth watchband—15
black anything—5
tan anything—5
brown purse or wallet—5
elastic on anything—15
pencil, not pen—15
5 pennies in purse or pocket—15

Players total their points. Now instruct them to deduct 5 points for each of the following they're wearing:

pants suit
gold earrings

safety pin anywhere
more than three rings
matches or lighter in purse or pocket
shoe heel higher than one inch
shoelaces
paper clip in purse or pocket
Player with the highest score wins.

100. Biographies. Each player is given a paper and pencil and told to write his name at the top of the paper. Then he is to number one through twenty down the left side. The leader instructs players to write down the following in consecutive order:

1. Any year
2. A town
3. Another town
4. Yes or no
5. Any number up to 20
6. An occupation or profession
7. Sum of money
8. Another sum of money
9. Descriptive adjective
10. A number
11. A color
12. Another color
13. Part of face or head
14. A bad habit
15. Sport or recreation
16. A flower
17. A vegetable
18. Exclamation or expletive
19. Length of life expected
20. Probable amount of estate

Papers are collected and the leader reads the biographies which may read something like this:

John Doe, born 1904, in New York, was educated in San Francisco. He is married and has seventeen children. His occupation is a launderer. His annual income is $12.00, his annual expenditure is $1,000. Personal appearance is strange, size of his shoes is twenty-four. His hair is green, eyes yellow, his mouth is his most handsome feature. His worst fault is blowing his nose too much. His favorite sport is bowling, his favorite flower is the goldenrod. His favorite vegetable is grapes. His favorite exclamation is "do say." He expects to live to be 100 and to leave an estate of five million dollars.

101. Bingo. Give out papers on which the letters B I N G O have been written and enough for each guest to have a square. (See example below.) Players are to get each guest's name in a square. When all have finished, leader calls out guests' names as players cross off on their papers the names that are called. Players to cross off all squares across in a line, all squares down in a line, or all squares diagonally, wins.

102. Songs, Sayings, Expressions. Give out papers on which the following has been written in a column:

Smile _____

Love _____

Heart _____

Day _____

Hand _____

Rain _____

Time _____

Night _____

Eye (s) _____

Rose _____

B	I	N	G	O

Leave space for players to write song titles, sayings and expressions using each word as many times as they can. Allow ten minutes playing time. Player with most answers wins.

103. Rhyming Synonyms. Give out papers with the column of words on the left written in. Opposite each word players are to write a rhyming word meaning the same thing. Example below.

    happy father—glad dad
    naughty boy—bad lad
    small skinny horse—bony pony
    antique seat—rare chair
    delicious fudge—dandy candy
    large hog—big pig
    small frankfurter—teeny weenie

fine orchestra—grand band
300-watt bulb—bright light or large charge
ordinary walking stick—plain cane
Saturday for school children—play day
overweight rodent—fat rat
smooth hen—slick chick
irritated employer—cross boss
comical rabbit—funny bunny
loafing flower—lazy daisy

104. Name the Animal. Give out papers numbered from one to thirty with the names in the left column written in. Instruct the players to write the name of the appropriate animal in the right column. Example below. Player with the most correct answers wins.

Animal	*Name the adult male*
	(Answers)
elephant	bull
dog	hound
deer	buck
buffalo	buck
hare	buck
sheep	ram
horse	stallion
cow	bull
antelope	buck
pig	boar

Animal	*Name the female*
	(Answers)
sheep	ewe
zebra	mare
fox	vixen

lion	lioness
elephant	cow
deer	doe
horse	mare
buffalo	cow
antelope	doe
hare	doe

Animal	*Name the baby*
	(Answers)
bear	cub
horse	colt or foal
cow	calf
buffalo	calf
dog	pup
deer	fawn
tiger	cub
sheep	lamb
elephant	calf
fox	cub

105. Match Mates. Give out papers numbered from one to fifteen. Beside each number write a name. In the center of the page leave a space for players to write the matching name from the column on the right. Example below.

Answers

1. David	Bathsheba	Edith
2. Romeo	Juliet	Beatrice
3. Tristan	Isolde	Betty
4. Archie	Edith	Martha
5. Jack Sprat	His wife	Jill

43

6.	Dante	Beatrice	Josephine
7.	John Alden	Priscilla	Priscilla
8.	Anthony	Cleopatra	Bathsheba
9.	Napoleon	Josephine	Mary Todd
10.	George	Martha	Cleopatra
11.	Jack	Jill	Isolde
12.	Abe	Mary Todd	His wife
13.	Aquila	Priscilla	Sarah
14.	Abraham	Sarah	Priscilla
15.	Jerry	Betty	Juliet

5

Games for Special Days

106. Up and Down. This game can be adapted to almost any occasion. Print the word "Valentine" twice vertically like below.

V	_____	E
A	_____	N
L	_____	I
E	_____	T
N	_____	N
T	_____	E
I	_____	L
N	_____	A
E	_____	V

Players are given ten or fifteen minutes in which to fill in letters in each line that will spell a word. A variation is to insist that players make only four letter words.

107. Baby Names. Instruct players to write down their mother's and father's first and last names vertically on a piece of paper. Players are then to write down a girl's name beginning with the letters in mother's name and a boy's name beginning with the letters of father's name. See example below. One point is given for each name no one else has. Player with most points wins.

J	(Josephine)	B	(Brian)
A	_____	I	_____
N	_____	L	_____
E	_____	L	_____
S	_____	S	_____
M	_____	M	_____
I	_____	I	_____
T	_____	T	_____
H	_____	H	_____

108. Scrambled Words. On the backs of penny valentines scramble words like those in the following column.

    teethearsw - sweetheart

    yenho - honey

    reda - dear

    ringlad - darling

    vole - love

    guh - hug

    skis - kiss

    missrope - promises

    palsrospo - proposals

    widnged singr - wedding rings

    korenb ratshe - broken hearts

    elvo lstreet - love letters

    gagmenneet ginrs - engagement rings

    rovesl squarrel - lovers quarrels

    ageirram ratle - marriage altar

Players are to unscramble the letters to make the words in the right column.

109. Real Estate. (This is more of a skit for a guest of honor than a game.) In advance give four men the following script to follow at a designated time.

A client walks up to a real estate broker and says, "I'd like to buy some land with something special, like an echo."

Agent: An echo?

Client: Yes, I want to be able to say anything and have the echo repeat it.

Agent: I have just the land for you. Let's go look at it now. (Both men take a few steps to another part of room.)

Agent: (Pointing with arm) Here it is. Speak in any direction and the echo will repeat what you say.

Client: Aw, baloney. I don't believe it.

Agent: Go ahead. Try it. Say something.

Client: (Cupping hand to mouth) Baloney.

Echo: (Standing just outside door) Baloney (softly).

Agent: Face in another direction and say something.

Client: Baloney.

Echo: Baloney.

Agent: Try it again. Face in another direction and say something.

Client: Baloney.

Echo: Baloney.

Agent: Try it facing in another direction. Say something different this time.

Client: Brother Jones is the best pastor in the whole world.

Echo: Baloney.

110. Words. Provide each player with a pencil and paper on which have been written the words Come As You Are

Party across the top. In a limited time, about twenty minutes, each player is to write a three or four letter word beginning with each letter in the words Come As You Are Party. Example below.

C—coat, car, cat, etc.
O—oar, omit, oat
M—met, map, mop
E—ear, era, easy

A—art, ate
S—some, same

Y—yet, your, yes
O—
U—

A—
R—
E—

P—
A—
R—
T—
Y—

111. Describe Sweetheart. Leader instructs players to write as many endearing words as they can in a given time to describe their sweethearts (or spouses). To be different, the player with the least number of words wins.

112. Word Association. Give each player pencil and paper.

Give each player one of the following words to write at the top of his paper: school, graduation, grade, test, class, classmate, boy, girl, job, college, high school, college degree, teacher, principal, pencil, sharpener, paper, pencil, pen, education, scholarship, book, schoolbook, textbook, notebook, English, math, history, freshman, junior, sophomore, senior. At a given signal for everyone give players five minutes to write the words he thinks of with each succeeding word. Read lists. Longest list wins.

113. Birthday Gift. Guest asks one person, "Do you have a gift for me?" That person says no but describes a person (personality traits or achievements, etc.) in the room who might have it. Everyone knows who actually has the group gift and he is not described until last. Guest then has to ask the person described until they allow him to guess the right one.

114. Telegram. Write a ten word telegram from a groom proposing marriage to a bride using the following letters as the first letter of each word in this order: I - W - R - M - Y - T - W - O - S - L.

115. Couples' Apparel. Write the groom's name at the head of one column and the bride's name at the head of another column. Under each name write an article of clothing beginning with the letters in each name. Give a prize for the funniest.

116. Predictions. Make small slips of paper to fold up for contestants to draw out of a box. On half of the papers put the bride's name; on the other half put the groom's name. Each person is told to draw a name and write a prediction for that person for the next ten years. All are to be read. Prize is given for the funniest.

117. Happy Marriage. Give pencil and paper to everyone. On the paper should have been written the word "Marriage" in a column at the left twice. In the first word players should write something husbands should never do using the letters in the word, such as below.

Husbands should never
M—Make fun of their wives' cooking
A
R
R
I
A
G
E

Wives should always
M—Make her husband comfortable
A
R
R
I
A
G
E

The leader, or new bride if it's a bridal shower, should select the most original.

118. Love and Marriage. Give out paper and pencil. Instruct players to write the words "Love and Marriage" at the top. Then they are to write as many words as they can using only the letters in "Love and Marriage." Proper names and foreign words may not be used. Player with the most words wins.

119. What Is Baby Made Of? Give out papers on which you have numbered and listed the words below in a column at the left. (Answers are in column at right.) Each word represents something a baby is made of. Players are to write the answer next to each word. Players may be given the first answer as an example.

		Answers
1.	Something to keep tools in	chest
2.	Part of a wagon	tongue
3.	Grown on a cornstalk	ears
4.	A type of macaroni	elbow
5.	A school child	pupil
6.	Tropical trees	palm
7.	Part of an apple	skin
8.	Edge of a saw	teeth
9.	Used by carpenters	nails
10.	Weapons of war	arms
11.	Part of a clock	face
12.	What dogs bury	bones
13.	Part of a bed	head
14.	Two sailors answering yes	ayes (eyes)
15.	Branches of a tree	limbs
16.	Opposite the head	foot
17.	A cad	heel
18.	What a wrecking car does	tows (toes)
19.	The biggest part of a giraffe	neck
20.	Place of worship	temple
21.	Top of a hill	brow

22. Weathercocks   vanes (veins)
23. What you put to the wheel   shoulder
24. The edge of a cup or glass   lip
25. What the tortoise raced
     with   hare (hair)
26. Part of a river   mouth
27. What you should keep out
     of other peoples' business   nose
28. A clam   mussel (muscle)
29. Used on Valentine's Day   heart
30. When two pipes are joined   joint
31. Used to cross a river   bridge
32. Used to hail a ride   thumb
33. A term applied to a
     football player   back
34. What we think with   brain
35. An entrance   arch
36. Part of an umbrella   ribs
37. Another term for blouse   waist
38. Sometimes it locks   jaw
39. A type of watch   wrist
40. A young cow   calf

6

Forfeits

1. Say three complimentary things about yourself.
2. Answer truthfully four questions asked by anyone.
3. Place one hand where the other hand can't reach it. (Elbow)
4. Make a speech on Women's Lib.
5. Blindfold two players in opposite corners and have them come forward, meet, and shake hands.
6. Leave room with two legs and come back with six. (Carrying chair.)
7. Pose as a statue.
8. Imitate three barnyard noises.
9. Hold ankle with hand and walk around the room.
10. Give an imitation of Rip Van Winkle waking up.
11. Lie down on the floor, fold arms, and get up without unfolding them.
12. Recite six lines of poetry while holding a nut or a piece of candy in your mouth.
13. Wrestle with temptation.
14. Say the alphabet backwards.
15. Propose to yourself and accept yourself.
16. Blow out a candle while blindfolded.
17. Say six nice things about yourself.
18. Confess your worst fault.
19. Imitate a traffic cop on a busy corner.
20. From a saucer of flour pick up a dime with your lips and without using your hands.

7

Special Programs

This Is Your Life

To present a This Is Your Life program you will need the assistance of the wife or mother if the program is for your pastor, for instance.

When the date has been selected, ask the pastor's wife for a list of all the people and their addresses (and their relationship) who had a significant part in his life. This would include family, friends, colleagues, teachers and professors, etc.

Then prepare a mimeographed letter to all on the above list. The suggested letter below may be adapted for your needs.

Date
Return Address

Dear Friend:

A SURPRISE This Is Your Life program is being presented for Rev. John Jones, pastor at (name of church and address). His wife, (wife's name), knows about the program.

This Is Your Life will be presented in the sanctuary of his church (date and time). You are cordially invited to attend.

We are asking each person who receives this letter to

write a letter to John Jones. But do not send it to him! Send it to the writer of this letter at the above address. In your letter to Rev. Jones write anything that is meaningful to you and him. It may be funny or serious or both. All of the letters received will go in a book to be presented the night of the program. Some (all) of the letters will be read aloud at the program. Your letter should be mailed no later than (date) to appear in the book.

If you have any pictures of our pastor that you are willing to part with, we'd like them to go in the book, too.

Write to me at the above address or phone me at (number) no later than (date) to let us know whether you will be able to attend.

Some of our church families would be happy to have you stay with them if you will be overnight guests. Or, if you prefer, motel reservations can be made for you. Let us know which you desire.

All who receive this letter and plan to attend are asked to meet at (time and place) before the program so that we can go to the church in a group. Provisions will be made for the group to enter the church and go to a private room without being seen by the pastor.

During the reading of the narrative at the program, you will make your appearance as your name is read.

We sincerely hope you will be able to attend and share this time with our pastor.

Remember to keep it a surprise.

Sincerely,
Jane Doe

The next step is a task of the pastor's wife. Ask her to jot down any or all of the following as she thinks of them. Give her a deadline for completing it. She may also give photographs or other memorabilia (programs, invitations, etc.) to be dated and included in chronological order in the book with that of the relatives and friends, etc.

Pastor's parents' names. Date and place of their marriage and who performed the ceremony if significant.

Pastor's place and date of birth and any interesting details or circumstances about it.

Names and ages of brothers and sisters. Their birth dates.

Names and relationship of other close family members.

Places pastor lived while growing up.

Grammar school he attended. Any interesting incidents involving school, teachers, classmates, average grades, etc.

Interesting events in his life such as a dog he had, daring things or mischievous things he did, clubs he joined, trouble he got into, his reaction to parental discipline, hobbies, exciting birthdays or Christmases, etc.

Date and circumstances concerning his decision to accept Christ.

High school he attended. Interesting events.

History of how and when he met his wife and later began dating.

History of courtship.

Details about engagement and wedding. Date, place, attendants, etc.

Humorous or interesting events of honeymoon.

College and seminary attended. Interesting events.

Name and date of each child's birth.

Interesting or funny struggles of marriage.

Circumstances concerning decision to become a minister.

Names and places and dates of churches he served as pastor.

Anything in his life that he would think was significant and anything that would be interesting or humorous to his congregation.

Don't be modest about his accomplishments.

When all material has been received from the pastor's wife, relatives, friends, etc. it is ready to be put in book form.

A large three-ring, looseleaf book should be purchased. The cover may be printed with the words This Is Your Life, John Jones.

A person with a flair for writing should put in narrative form all the information collected from the pastor's wife. Information should be written in chronological order beginning with his birth, and double-spaced. This would appear first in the book.

Following this would be all the letters in order of their appearance in the narrative. (Everyone sending a letter should be mentioned in the narrative. Others may appear in the narrative who fail to send letters.)

Following the letters would be the photographs in chronological order.

To make the book a permanent keepsake, narrative, letters and pictures may be placed between acetate pages available at office supply stores.

At the time of the program, the pastor may come to the church on any pretext his wife chooses.

One person should serve as master of ceremonies, welcome those in attendance and begin reading the narrative. At this time the pastor is asked to come forward and take a seat of honor. As each person is mentioned in the narrative, he should come forward and be recognized by the pastor. (Those from out of town should remain in another room, or hall, until the time of their appearance in the narrative.) When each person is mentioned in the narrative and comes forward, his letter should be read if there aren't too many and if time permits.

A suggested beginning for the narrative is below.

December 30, 1925, Jane Doe and John Jones were married in Lexington, Kentucky. Their first (second, third) child, John Jones, Jr., was born November 1, 1926. This is your life, John Jones!

John, do you remember the house where you were born? It was. . .

This program is usually considered an honor.

Refreshments may be served afterward.

Pastor's Resignation

Dining Area Scene:

(A good time to present this program would be following a dinner in the pastor's honor.)

Officer: (Wears large badge. Stands outside dining area.) (Knocks loudly) Open up in the name of the law.

Church Member No. 1: (Getting up from table) I'll go see who it is.

Officer: (Stepping inside dining area) I have a subpoena for Rev. and Mrs. John Jones.

Church Member No. 1: (Pointing) There they are.

Officer: (Addressing Rev. and Mrs. Jones) This is a court

citation ordering Rev. and Mrs. John Jones to appear before Judge I. M. Impartial of (name of church) Court, when his court convenes in the chapel in ten minutes, to answer to the charges brought by Mr. Highly Disappointed and Mr. I. Will Missyou who represent the entire membership of (name of church).

Church Member No. 2: Well, they've got it coming.

Church Member No. 3: Boy, the judge will straighten them out. (Everyone leaves dining area and goes to chapel.) COURT ROOM SCENE: (Mr. Highly Disappointed, Mr. I. Will Missyou, prosecuting attorney, defense attorney and clerk are seated on stage. Officer keeps Rev. and Mrs. Jones in auditorium.)

Clerk: (After noticing that everyone is seated, rises) Please rise. (Motions to audience) The Honorable Judge I. M. Impartial is entering the courtroom. (Judge enters and is seated.)

Clerk: Please be seated.

Judge: (Pounding gavel) The court will please come to order. (Looking at clerk) Read the case for the court.

Clerk: Your Honor, the case today is the membership of (name of church), represented by Mr. Highly Disappointed and Mr. I. Will Missyou, against Rev. and Mrs. John Jones for leaving (name of church) without permission.

Judge: Call the defendants, Rev. and Mrs. John Jones, to the stand. (Waits until they are seated. Looking at prosecuting attorney) Proceed with the case, Mr. Prosecuting Attorney.

Prosecuting Attorney: Your Honor and Ladies and Gentlemen, the defendants, Rev. and Mrs. John Jones, have made a final and irrevocable commitment to another church, leaving (name of church) without a pastor.

59

This charge, alone, would be enough grounds for prosecution, but added to that charge is the fact that they are leaving without knowing how much they are loved, how much their leadership has meant and many other things the membership has not made them realize. In view of these circumstances my clients, Mr. Highly Disappointed and Mr. I. Will Missyou, feel the defendants, Rev. and Mrs. Jones should be compelled to remain at (name of church) another few years until freed of the charge of leaving without permission.

Judge: How do the defendants reply to the charge of leaving without permission?

Defense Attorney: Your Honor, the defendants were subpoenaed just a few minutes ago and I have not had time to confer with them. However, since the membership of (name of church) appointed me to be the defense attorney, I will proceed. The defendants are known by the entire membership to be sincerely dedicated to the tasks which God has set before them to do. For this reason, alone, it is clear to see why Mr. Highly Disappointed and Mr. I. Will Missyou would seem to have a case. As their names imply, they are disappointed because the defendants are leaving and they will miss them. But the membership must bear in mind that they have had (number) enriching years under the leadership of the defendants—(number) years in which their individual lives, as well as the church, have been blessed. During all this time, as leaders at (name of church), Rev. and Mrs. Jones never once committed an act or uttered a word which could in any way have been detrimental to God's work. During their (number) year tenure they did do and say everything within their power to make (name of church) and its members a church God would be pleased to bless. By their dedicated, humble Christian example they have endeared themselves to every member of the church. It is indeed understandable that their leaving will mean a great loss to (name of church)—a loss and emptiness that no other person can fill. But I urge Mr. Highly Disappointed, Mr. I. Will Missyou and the membership they represent to call to mind the one thing they admire most about the defendants: their dedication in fulfilling the will of God. The defendants, Rev. and Mrs. Jones, have little regard for the insignificant subpoena and decision of this court. They honor the decision and will of a higher court, a nobler Judge. For this reason I beseech the membership of (name of church) to withdraw their charge of leaving without permission and ask them to pray God's blessings on the defendants as they answer the call of the most high Judge to accept the challenge of entering and serving a new church where they don't know yet what problems they will meet and what rewards they will reap. Out of love for the defendants I think the membership of (name of church) should want to change their charge from that of leaving without permission to that of leaving with the prayer for God's blessings.

Judge: Has the prosecuting attorney anything to say in summation?

Prosecuting Attorney: Your Honor, my clients want it to go on record that they were represented by Mr. Highly Disappointed and Mr. I. Will Missyou because this is how they truly feel. However, after hearing the defense, they realize how selfish they have been in wanting Rev. and Mrs. Jones to stay. They further realize they have been negligent in not seeking, through prayer, the will of the highest court. My clients withdraw their charge and resolve to keep in their hearts a special love for the defendants and in the future strive to help make (name of church) the kind of church the defendants have prayed it would be.

Judge: Inasmuch as the charge has been withdrawn and a change of heart has been made manifest, it is the decision of this court that the defendants, Rev. and Mrs. Jones, leave if they must, but take with them the knowledge that our love and our prayers go with them.

(Presenting a gift or singing Blest Be the Tie would be appropriate.)

(A scroll with words similar to those below would be appropriate to present to the pastor and his wife.)

Resolution

Whereas, we believe that our church is directed by the divine leadership of God insofar as we, as church members, allow it to be; and

Whereas, we prayerfully desire to continue to be led by God; and

Whereas, we accept God's will even when we do not always understand his reasons; and

Whereas, we regret losing our inspired leader sent from God; therefore,

Resolved, That we shall, through prayer, seek God's will for the continuation of this church.

Resolved, That, as Rev. and Mrs. Jones leave us to go to another church, we will pray for God's blessings on them and their family and on their work for God to which they have dedicated their lives.

(Date)   Membership   (Name of church)

New Member Shower

One way to encourage new members to feel at home at church and to get to know other members is to have a New Member Shower.

About five weeks before the New Member Shower, notice of a churchwide social, without details, could be put in the church paper or announced. This is done so that people would not schedule anything else for that evening. Two weeks before the shower, an invitation (suggestion below) should be put in the church paper.

Announcement

Everyone at (name of church) is cordially invited to a New Member Shower Friday night, October 3, 7:30 to 9:00 P.M. in fellowship hall.

Instead of buying gifts for all the new members who have joined (name of church) during the past year, we will shower them with paper slips. On a slip of paper or small card write something that has helped you to grow spiritually that you would like to share with a new member. You might want to write a Bible verse, or the title and author of a book, or a song title, or the name of a Christian friend, or the title or date of one of the pastor's sermons, or . . . anything you like. You may sign your name if you like but it isn't necessary. These spiritual helps will be dropped into a basket and given to new members at the shower.

For your pleasure and enrichment there will be:
    A style show featuring some of our men
    Singing
    Introduction of the ministerial staff
    Opportunities to meet new members
    Youth to age twelve provided for in another room
    Testimonials

Sandwiches and drinks
Nursery

Come to the shower, have fun, and meet new members of (name of church) Friday night, October 3, 7:30 to 9:00 P.M.

At the same time a similar invitation on cards should be mailed to all members who have joined the church within the past year.

The ceiling of fellowship hall could be decorated with many rain drops cut from colored construction paper and hung by threads with transparent tape. Large umbrellas cut from construction paper and outlined with felt tip pens could be hung on the walls and from the ceiling. Small umbrellas cut from construction paper, outlined with felt tip pens and with pipe stem cleaner handles could be made for name tags. As each person arrives he should be given a name tag to fill out and pin on. A large umbrella decorated with long stem artificial roses could be placed at each end of the refreshment table.

The first fifteen minutes could be spent talking with other members while waiting for latecomers. Then everyone should sit in chairs on each side of the hall facing a runway down the center made of wide paper taped to the floor. Program might be as follows:

Welcome by Master or Mistress of Ceremonies.

Introduction of ministerial staff. (The following was used at the writer's church and may be adapted. To be sung to the tune of Frankie and Johnnie.)

Listen here all you new members,
Pay heed and please do not laugh,
We'll give you all of the lowdown
On the ministerial staff

64

That leads us here
At Immanuel Church.

First take the case of our pastor,
He's known to all as Ted Sisk,
He preaches long in the pulpit,
And you listen at your own risk,
You can't turn him off,
He goes on and on.

Each sermon he does deliver
He uses the Bible as text,
He pours it on all those sinners
And you know that you'll be next,
He raves against
All your favorite sins.

Bill Williams leads choir rehearsals,
Teaching the ohs, ahs, and loos,
Helping choir members sing anthems
To the people in the pews,
Allelujah
And amen.

Bill also leads Sunday mornings,
He tells us what we will sing,
Page 44 is the number
Let the joists and rafters ring,
We're all on key,
We don't dare be flat.

Now let me introduce Billy.
Siress is his last name,
He makes directors work harder,
Compared to him Simon Legree is tame,
Read this, read that,
Learn to do it right.

Billy will visit you teachers,
Some Sunday morning, it's true,
He'll watch your methods, procedures,
Then he'll raise his brow at you,
He'll enroll you
In a study course.

Andy Good rules our new building,
C L C, that is its name,
Crafts, sports, and fun he does schedule,
Christian living's the name of his game,
'Cause he's so tall
We look up to him.

He took the juniors to camp once,
They had a ball, played it cool,
He pushed the kids and the counselors
With their clothes on into the pool,
It took ten kids
To do the same to him.

Now that you've heard all the lowdown,
Seen what a staff we have here,
Let me just tell you one more thing,
I was never more sincere,
We love our staff
Just the way they are.

Staff members could be asked now to make one minute impromptu speeches.

This could be followed by all singing "Sweet, Sweet Spirit." (Mimeographed song sheets should be provided when people enter fellowship hall.)

Fun songs (from mimeographed sheet) could be sung by all. Suggestions: "When the Moon Comes Over the Mountain"; "Home, Home on the Range"; "She'll Be Comin'

Round the Mountain"; "The Little Brown Church"; "Oh, My Darling Clementine"; "Old MacDonald's Farm," etc.

There could be three to five minute testimonials from four new members.

New members now should walk to a flower-decorated basket on a table and select their shower gifts. A few minutes could be allowed for them to read them and share them with their neighbors back at their seats. (Pencils and paper should be provided at the table at the beginning of the shower for members who forgot to bring slips of paper.)

A style show with men dressed in women's clothing should follow.

Pastor could lead in prayer and all could again sing "Sweet, Sweet Spirit."

Refreshments.

Pastor Appreciation Time

The following may be adapted and used as an introduction of the pastor at any event honoring him such as Pastor Appreciation Time (hour, day, etc.)

Introduction

As chairman of the pulpit committee, I introduced your pastor to you (number) years ago. Let me introduce him to you again today.

John Jones is a son, a husband, a father, a Christian, a pastor, a friend, a teacher, and a (fast driver, foot tapper, anything light). I would not presume to place these titles of his in the order of their priority. However, I do know that as a Christian, John's first allegiance is to God and God's cause. His other roles fall into place as God allows him the time.

As a son he is adored by his mother and respected by his

father. They have lavished their time and love on him. As a result he is probably spoiled and conditioned to having his way with them. At the same time, he loves and respects his parents and probably feels God blessed him generously by making them his parents.

As a husband, John has had to learn to share and give-and-take, as all husbands must. With mutual love and trust and respect flowing between John and Jane, John knows the joy that comes with wedded bliss. Of course, he also knows the (worry, fear, etc.) that comes when Jane (mention a trait of hers that can be taken lightly).

As a father he knows the pride and joy one feels when looking into innocent faces and knowing they are a part of him and he is helping to mold them. And he knows the feeling of a swelled ego as his children let him know he's the greatest.

It's as pastor and friend, the two roles inseparable, that he's known best by most people. What kind of pastor and friend is John Jones?

The first word to describe him takes care of another of his roles. John is a Christian. As such, he strives in every way to be the kind of Christian, the kind of pastor, and the kind of friend Christ would have him be.

The basis for his preaching, service to mankind, and spiritual growth for his congregation is God's Word. He places his service to Christ, and to mankind in Christ's name, above personal recognition or goals. He accepts and carries out the tasks of his ministry with responsibility. He seeks to meet the needs of all who come his way and all he goes out of his way to find, loving and helping friend and stranger impartially. He remains mute regarding the shared confidences of others. He seeks to train lay workers in the church and helps build their confidence for the work.

He remains humble in praise and grateful in criticism. He leads rather than commands his flock, showing the way and setting the example. To the lost, he introduces Christ. To the sorrowing, he offers comfort. To the injured, he offers help. To the elated, he shares in their joy. To the troubled, he offers a solution. To all he offers empathy, compassion, love, and Christ's way. To fellow Christians he points the way to spiritual growth and a closer relationship with God.

To say that John Jones is special is not an overstatement, because to each of you he has filled a need in a special way. If you have experienced heights of joy, John has shared it with you. If you have known the depths of despair or trouble, John has been there to show you he cares. And even if these two poles-apart experiences have not been yours, John has been special to your life by just being himself—dependable, friendly, strong, and caring.

With all this praise about John, can we say he's perfect? No, we can't. And he would be the first to tell us he isn't. But he tries, and he tries hard to be the man, the pastor, the friend, God wants him to be.

I said I would introduce your pastor to you and that's what I've been leading up to. So, to put it very simply, I present to you God's chosen man in God's chosen place at God's chosen time doing God's chosen work—your pastor, John Jones!

After the pastor has been introduced, each member may come by to shake his hand and tell him how much he's appreciated.

This might be followed by the presentation of a gift from all the members, and refreshments.

8

Miscellaneous Games

Indoor Games

A. Who Has the Bell? Players stand or sit in a circle. Someone is selected as "It." He closes his eyes and counts aloud to ten. While he is doing this, players pass a small bell around. When "It" reaches eight or nine the bell stops passing and all players place their hands behind their backs. "It" tries to guess who has the bell. If he guesses correctly who is holding the bell, "It" changes places with the person caught. If not, the game continues with the same "It."

B. Candle Relay. The group is divided into two teams placed in parallel lines. The first player on each team has a candle and a book of matches. At a given signal the first member of each team lights his candle, runs with it to a designated goal, and returns, giving the lighted candle to the second team member. If the candle goes out while the player is running, he must stop and relight the candle before continuing.

C. Cotton Balls. Each player, in turn, stands at a starting point and throws a ball of cotton. Player throwing the cotton ball the farthest, wins.

D. Hum a Tune. Select one person to be "It" and stand him in the center of a circle of players. He is blindfolded and has a baton (ruler will do) with which he leads the group in singing a hymn they are familiar with. At any time during the singing, "It" may call out, "Stop." At that time he points his baton at a player in the circle who must hum the remainder of the hymn. "It" then tries to guess who is humming before he reaches the end of the hymn. If "It" guesses correctly he changes places with the hummer. If the group is small, you might limit "It" to only three guesses.

E. Ping-Pong Race. Divide group into two teams. Teams are lined up at a starting point. A chalk line (or string) is at goal line across the room. At a given signal the first person on each team gets down on the floor and using only a drinking straw to blow through, propels a Ping-Pong ball across the room. As one team member finishes, ball is brought back and given to next team member. Team finishing first wins.

F. Shoes Gone. All players remove their shoes and place them in a box. Hostess carries the box to the other end of the room. At a signal all players rush to find their shoes, put them on properly and go back to designated starting point. First player back wins.

G. Whose Lap? Guests should be seated in a circle. "It" should be blindfolded and in the center. "It" moves to someone's chair and sits down in his lap. He says, "Who are you?" The person whose lap "It" is sitting in says (disguising his voice any way he likes), "I can't tell you." "It" then guesses whose lap he is sitting on. If he guesses correctly they change places. If not, "It" tries again. During game players may exchange seats in an attempt to fool "It."

H. Hit the Dummy. One player is selected to be "It." He stands with his back to the other players. One player throws a soft, small pillow and hits "It." "It" turns then and tries to guess who hit him. If he guesses correctly he changes places with that person. If he guesses incorrectly, he remains "It."

I. Feather Blowing. Divide players into two teams and give each team a small feather. Each team is to toss its feather into the air and, with hands held behind their backs, try to keep the feather in the air by blowing. Team to keep the feather in the air the longest time wins.

J. Chin the Apple. Players are divided into two teams of equal number. The first person of each team is given an apple which he places under his chin. He is to pass the apple to the next team member, under the chin, without either of them using their hands. If the apple is dropped, the player who dropped it picks it up, places it back under his chin and begins again. Game continues until one team is finished and wins.

K. Occupation. Divide group into small groups of about five each (depending on size). Each small group draws from a box a slip of paper with the name of an occupation written on it. Each small group acts out the occupation while the others try to guess what it is.

L. X Marks the Spot. In advance leader tapes a piece of white adhesive tape with a red X on a player's arm and tells him to remain quiet about it. The group is then told to hunt a red X on a small white square which is in plain sight. When players locate it they are to say nothing and sit down. Others, including the one wearing the red X, continue the search. Game ends when all have located the spot or given up.

M. Dime Pick Up. Divide group into two teams of equal number. Place a small table in front of each team. On each table is a plate of four dimes and a pair of work gloves (or rubber gloves). The first person of each team, at a given signal, puts on the gloves, picks up the dimes and places them on the table. The second person of each team then puts on the gloves and places the dimes back in the plate. The third person puts on the gloves and places the dimes back on the table. Game continues in this manner until all members of one team have picked up the dimes. That team wins.

N. Personal Treasure Hunt. The group should be divided into two teams of equal number. A leader and scorekeeper are needed. Each team should be lined up behind an empty chair. The leader will call out an article from his list. The first person on each team is to run to his team members, see if they have the article, then run and place it on his team's chair. The team leader who places an article on the chair first receives a point for his team. To determine which team wins, scores are totaled. List of personal items may include a hairpin, a two dollar bill, a red hair, a gray hair, an emerald (imitation) ring, a penny, a shoe with a buckle, a size 7½ shoe, a class ring, a baby picture, a tissue, etc.

O. Life Savers. Divide group into two teams of equal

number. Supply the first person of each team with a Life Saver and supply each player with a toothpick. At a given signal the first person of each team places his Life Saver on his toothpick which is held firmly with his teeth. The first person passes his Life Saver from his toothpick to the toothpick of the next in line, and so on down the line. No hands may touch the Life Saver or the toothpick. When every member on a team has successfully passed the Life Saver, that team wins.

P. Non-Weight Lifting. Each player is to take his turn at being blindfolded and led to a table where there is a bowl of five or six cotton balls. Using a tablespoon each player, in turn, is to pick up the cotton balls out of the bowl and put them on the table. When each player finishes, the leader places the cotton balls back into the bowl and the next player tries.

Q. Beans or Peas. Divide group into two teams of equal number. Place a chair, on which has been placed a saucer with four dried beans (or peas) and an empty saucer, in front of each team. At a given signal the first person of each team is to kneel or stoop, pick up the four beans in his saucer by using a straw placed in his mouth, and transfer the beans to the empty saucer. The next person in line does the same thing. The first team to finish placing the four beans in a saucer, wins.

Outdoor Games
R. Laugh at the Handerchief. Players form a circle and the leader stands in the center. Leader tosses a handkerchief into the air. While it is floating down everyone must laugh. When the handkerchief touches the floor, all players must

74

stop laughing entirely. Players who laugh when they are not supposed to or who do not laugh when they are supposed to are out of the game. They may try to make players still in the game laugh at the wrong time.

S. Banana Peel. Each player is given a banana which he is to peel and eat, keeping one hand behind him. All start at the same time. The one who finishes first wins.

T. Balloon Aloft. Players are divided into two teams with a starting point (tree, rock, or whatever) and a goal line designated. Each team is given a balloon. The first person on each team is to take his balloon to the goal line and back and give it to the next team member. The balloon may not be held nor may it drop to the ground. It must be kept aloft by the player batting it and keeping it in the air as he moves toward the goal and back. The team which finishes first wins.

U. Cup of Water. Each player is given a small paper cup half filled with water which he is to hold in his teeth, kneel on both knees, and drink all the water without touching the cup with his hands.

V. Curb or Street. All players form a circle around someone selected to be "It." If "It" calls, "In the street," all players must step one step into the center of the circle. If "It" calls, "On the curb," players must step back one step if they are "in the street." Players are out of the game if they step ahead when they are already in the street or if they step back when they are already on the curb. "It" may try to confuse the players by his word signals. Game continues until only one player is left.

W. Kick Backward. Instruct players to see which one can kick a ball (football, soccer, basketball) farthest by kicking the ball so that it goes back over his head rather than forward.

X. Fly Swatter. "It" stands in the center of other players who form a circle. A large box is placed in the center of the circle. "It" has a roll of newspaper in his hand, chooses someone in the circle and swats him with the newspaper. "It" places the newspaper roll in the box. The person swatted runs and grabs the newspaper and tries to swat "It" before "It" can take his place in the circle. If "It" gets in the vacant place before being swatted, the other person becomes "It." If the player swats "It" before he gets to the vacant place, then "It" goes back into the circle and swats someone else as the game continues.

Y. Ice Cubes. Players should be divided into two teams of equal number (about five or six). Each team is given an ice cube which they must pass from one member to another, keeping the ice moving, but not letting it fall to the ground. Players may rub the ice in their hands or even on their clothing but may not put it into their mouths. The team whose ice cube melts first wins.

Z. Barnyard. The group is divided into two teams of equal number. A farmer (leader) is selected for each team. Other members are the farm animals. Each team has a designated starting point and a "water trough" (tree or other object). At a given signal the farmer of each team grabs one of his animals and takes it to the water trough, circles it, and goes back to the starting point. Together they take another animal to the trough and back, circling the trough each time.

All going to the water trough must hold hands even when the line gets long as they circle the trough. The farmer that takes all of his animals to the trough, adding one each time, wins.

Pencil and Paper Games

AA. Notice This. After players have been in the room for a while, send them all into another room. While they are gone, rearrange items and furniture in the room as much as possible. Write down the changes. Ask players to return to the room and write down all the changes they notice. Player with the longest list wins.

BB. Eight Kates. Give a piece of paper to each guest on which has been mimeographed the following questions (answers are in parenthesis; do not mimeograph them):

1. What Kate is always repeating herself? (duplicate)
2. What Kate makes wheels go round? (lubricate)
3. What Kate is always making speeches at ceremonies for the opening of new buildings? (dedicate)
4. What Kate chews her food well? (masticate)
5. What Kate is always out of breath? (suffocate)
6. What Kate is full of advice? (advocate)
7. What Kate is good at finding things? (locate)
8. What Kate is able to get out of difficult situations? (extricate)

CC. Fancy Attire. After all members are together, have one person, elaborately overdressed, appear and walk around the room so that all guests may see him clearly. When he leaves, ask players to write down as many articles of clothing and their decriptions that they can recall seeing on the overdressed member.

DD. Letter M. In advance hang magazine pictures about the room. When guests arrive they are given pencil and paper and instructed to name, in a given time, all the objects in the pictures that begin with the letter "M." Pictures may be numbered and players may put the names of the objects to corresponding numbers on their papers. Player with longest list wins.

EE. Guess What. As players are seated pass around a large sack that you have prepared beforehand. In the sack are about thirty household items such as eggbeater, sponge, bottle opener, bottle cap, etc. As soon as each player has had an opportunity to feel the items in the sack (he may not look), instruct players to write down as many objects as they can remember. Player with the longest list wins.